The Incas

Macdonald Educational

C.A. Burland

The Incas

The Incas were not a tribe, nor were they a nation. They were a family who originally ruled a small mountain domain in present-day Peru. Little by little, they extended their empire until by the end of the 15th century it covered an area over 3,000 kilometres in length.

At its height the Inca civilization was a model of social organization. Everyone, from the Emperor at the top to the peasant farmer at the bottom, knew his place in society and the work he was expected to do. It was a period of great achievements. Splendid cities and buildings were constructed, many of them perched precariously on remote mountainsides. A network of roads, often carved through mountains, linked up towns throughout the empire. And despite an ever-growing population, an efficient system of agriculture ensured that there was always enough food for everybody.

Craftsmen too played an important part in Inca civilization. Skilled weavers wove fine and distinctive textiles, potters made jars and vases to traditional designs, while metalworkers fashioned fabulous objects in gold and silver to adorn palaces and temples.

But in 1532 Pizarro and a small group of Spanish soldiers landed in Peru, lured by tales of vast hoards of gold. Helped by a civil war amongst the Incas, the Spaniards soon succeeded in overcoming the natives. They administered the country as a Spanish feudal province. Gradually all the old Inca traditions were lost.

Fortunately Spanish priests later collected historical tales, and wrote them down. Thanks to their writing and to archaeological evidence, we can piece together the fascinating story of the highest civilization of ancient America.

Contents

Festival of the Sun

► After the solemn ritual is over, the people will dance and sing to the music of panpipes, flutes and drums.

▼ The Sapa Inca, his wife at his side, blesses the white llama before driving it off to the mountains to die. Surrounding the Inca are other important members of the Inca family, dressed in their finest clothes. Less important people look on respectfully from a distance.

For 500 years the Indians of Peru had known that a family called the Incas ruled in the mountain town of Cuzco and that their chief the Sapa Inca was descended from Inti, the Sun god. Later when the Incas ruled almost all the Andean area, every tribe accepted the Sapa Inca as a divine King. The Inca insisted that every tribe in the empire should build a temple to the Sun god. But the chief Sun temple was in the capital at Cuzco. Here on the day when the sun passed overhead at noon the people celebrated their New Year Festival, led by the Sapa Inca.

At the time of the great Sun Festival all the non-Inca people left Cuzco. They camped in the fields outside the town. The rest of the population gathered in the square near the temple. Inside the holy building the Inca took off his crown (a simple head-band with a sacred symbol in front) and prayed to the Sun all night. Then as the rays of the rising sun filled the temple, he came out into the square and welcomed a pure white llama. He spoke to the animal and gave it a message to give to the gods. It was then driven out into the mountains to die and take its message to the Sun.

Then the people began to celebrate because the Sapa Inca had called on the gods to bless the land. Musicians played and the people danced and drank *chicha* (beer made from maize). At every town in the empire there was a festive dance to the Sun, but at the same time the whole nation remembered that the Sapa Inca was the child of the Sun. He ruled them for their good, just as the Sun made the plants grow and the animals prosper.

9

The land

The Incas ruled a mountainous land a little larger than modern Peru. The highland making up most of the empire consists of two parallel mountain ranges with high plateaux, basins and deep valleys. Much of it is over 3,000 metres above sea level. Here the easterly winds blow over the great Amazon jungles, losing their rain as they rise to the great mountain ranges.

Beyond the coastal ranges no rain falls at all. The coastlands are a terrible desert through which a few short, torrential rivers cut their way to the sea. The coastal climate is affected by the cold Humboldt current flowing up the coast, which causes mist to hang over the desert, cooling it for many months of the year.

Peruvian life was based in the coastlands on fishing and on the plateaux on agriculture and animal breeding. The heavily-forested Amazon valley supplied tropical fruit, animal skins and brilliant feathers.

Amazon Basin

Pacific Ocean

▶ A section across Peru from west to east, showing how the rainfall is distributed across the land.

▼ The arid coastal desert near the Moche valley in Northern Peru. Vegetation grows only in the river valleys.

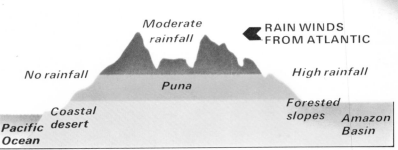

Moderate rainfall

◀ RAIN WINDS FROM ATLANTIC

No rainfall

High rainfall

Puna

Coastal desert

Forested slopes

Amazon Basin

Pacific Ocean

▼ Peru is dominated by the great mountain ranges of the Andes. The Inca capital, Cuzco, was situated on the high plateau at 3500 metres above sea level. There were vast climatic differences between the cold high plateaux, the hot, wet rainforests of the Amazon Basin and the hot, dry coastal desert.

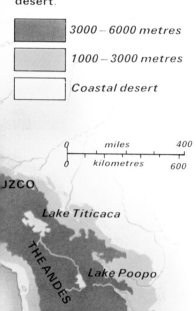

3000 – 6000 metres

1000 – 3000 metres

Coastal desert

miles   400
0
0
kilometres   600

JZCO

Lake Titicaca

THE ANDES

Lake Poopo

▲ Machu Picchu, one of the most impressive of the Inca highland towns. Terraces were built on the slopes for crops.

▼ The cold, high plains between the mountain ranges were the natural home of herds of llamas, alpacas and vicunas.

The people

The Peruvians were American Indians, with brown skins, brown eyes and straight black hair. They had first moved into the area as small tribes of hunters, but gradually over thousands of years built up the finest civilizations of the American Indian race.

Between 900 to 200 BC on the northern highlands and coast they formed the Chavin culture, which developed into a variety of regional cultures. From 100 BC to AD 600 the Mochica culture flourished on the north coast, with its great pyramids and fine pottery, while on the southern coast the Paracas culture had developed into the Nazca culture. In the highlands the people around Lake Titicaca built an important city at Tiahuanaco. Some said the Incas descended from these southern highland peoples, but they probably came from near Cuzco.

After AD 1100 the Chimu people on the south coast ruled the most powerful of the coastal states, while slowly the Inca family developed their civilization in the highlands at Cuzco. At first they ruled only the one town, but when jealous neighbours attempted to attack them, they resisted and gradually began to defeat the surrounding tribes. By the end of the 15th century the Incas ruled a vast empire extending to the coasts and from Ecuador to the River Maule in Chile. They called it *Tahuantinsuyu*, which means the Four Quarters (of the World).

▲ A gold mask from the early Nazca civilization, dating from about AD 100. It was found on a mummy buried in the coastal sands.

▼ The Chimu capital city Chanchan, seen from the air. Built about AD 1200-1300, it was a rich and powerful city covering some 28 sq km.

◄ These Indian boys of Peru looking through a window of an Inca ruin near Cuzco, are descended from the people of the Inca heartland. Although they speak Spanish at school, they still speak Quechua, the Inca language, at home.

► A pottery vase from the Mochica civilization of coastal Peru. These artistic people lived between 100 BC and AD 600.

► A giant stone statue from the ancient ruins of Tiahuanaco. It dates from about AD 700.

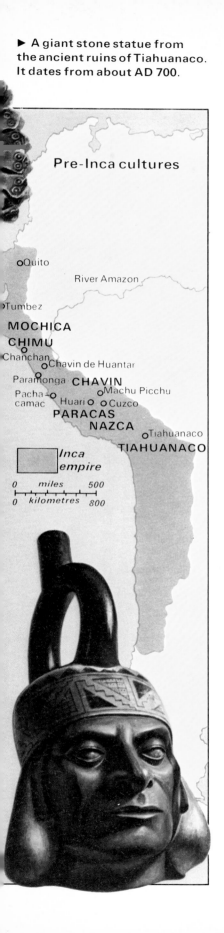

Pre-Inca cultures

○Quito

River Amazon

○Tumbez

MOCHICA
CHIMU
○
Chanchan
○Chavin de Huantar
Paramonga
CHAVIN
○Machu Picchu
Pacha-○
camac ○Huari ○ ○Cuzco
PARACAS
NAZCA
○Tiahuanaco
TIAHUANACO

Inca empire

0   miles   500
0 kilometres 800

13

Conquest!

▼ Topa Inca Yupanqui urges his men on to battle against the Chimu defenders of Paramonga. The large gold disc he is wearing on his chest is a military award; lesser awards were made from bronze and silver. Topa Inca is carrying a star-headed mace, a favourite Inca weapon.

Topa Inca Yupanqui, Pachacuti Inca's son and heir, was the greatest of all the Inca warriors. Under his leadership the Inca empire expanded rapidly. One of his most important victories was the conquest, in about AD 1450, of the powerful Chimu kingdom on the Pacific coast.

The Inca armies took the Chimu by surprise by attacking the Paramonga fortress in the south of their kingdom while the main Chimu army was defending the easier country in the north. They descended on the fortress with trumpets blaring and drums beating. All the soldiers joined in deafening and boastful songs.

▼ The Paramonga fortress was constructed around a natural hill of rock. This was built up by massive layers of mud bricks in several stages. The bricks were not baked but simply dried in the sun, for there was hardly any rain to damage them. At the top of each stage of the fortress was a fighting space, protected by a low wall. The Paramonga fortress covered the coastal roads towards the Chimu cities.

The Inca soldiers wielded spears with bronze blades, war clubs with spiked heads of bronze, and slings which threw egg-shaped stones with great force. The stones flew so fast that it was hard to dodge them, so the warriors' bodies were protected by tunics made of several layers of quilted cloth. They wore wooden or quilted cotton helmets on their heads and round shields of protective armour on their backs.

The Chimu hurled great boulders down on the attacking soldiers, who continued to advance on the fortress under the protection of great sheets of tough cotton, covering about 100 men. The defenders also used long spears to push down the Incas but finally they were driven back from wall to wall until at the top the last few survivors surrendered.

The Sapa Inca

► The Inca being shown a model of a building by its architect. The man on the left is recording information on special knotted strings called a quipu.

◄ The Inca's meals were served in bowls of gold and finest pottery. He ate alone and his quarters were guarded at all times.

The title Sapa Inca really means 'The Only Emperor'. He was the child of the Sun. When he took the throne he had to marry his eldest sister, who was called the Coya (Queen). Their first son would in turn become the next Inca. The Emperor could also have many other wives, but any children he had by them were not entitled to inherit his position.

The Sapa Inca was an absolute ruler. He might choose advisers to help him solve problems, but his own word was law. He had to approve plans for all battles undertaken in his name. No towns or buildings could be built without his permission. Frequent visits from provincial governors and administrators kept him in touch with what was going on everywhere in his empire. He himself travelled a great deal to visit his people though he remained aloof and unapproachable at all times.

Every Sapa Inca built his own palace in the centre of Cuzco, from which he ruled. Here he was surrounded by fine objects specially made for him and waited on hand and foot by his many wives. When he died his body was preserved and kept in the palace, where attendants continued to look after him as they had throughout his life.

▲ The Sapa Inca and his family. They all wore clothes woven specially for them by the Sun Virgins. The Inca wore a special headdress with a red woollen fringe over his forehead. In his ears he had great golden discs. These earplugs could only be worn by people of Inca descent.

► Once a year, the mummified body of a dead Inca was dressed in his finest clothes and carried in a solemn procession to the Sun temple.

THE INCA DYNASTY

Sometime after AD 1100 the Inca family arrived at Cuzco. They were led by **Manco Capac** *(AD ?)*

Sinchi Roca *(AD ?)*

Lloque Yupanqui *(AD ?)*

Mayta Capac *(AD ?)*. Under him the Incas occupied the whole of the city of Cuzco.

Capac Yupanqui

Inca Roca. In this period Inca armies raided the coastal towns.

Yahuar Huacac

Viracocha Inca

Inca Urcon

Pachacuti Inca Yupanqui *(AD 1438-71)* captured the whole highland area of Peru.

Topa Inca Yupanqui *(AD 1471-93)* was a great warrior who captured the coastal regions and sailed out to Pacific islands.

Huayna Capac *(AD 1493-1525)* conquered the kingdom of Quito and extended the empire as far as the Rio Maule in Chile. He divided his empire between his sons Huascar and Atahuallpa. This led to civil war.

Huascar *(AD 1525-32)* was made Sapa Inca but was defeated in battle by Atahuallpa.

Atahuallpa *(AD 1532-33)* usurped Huascar's position, but was captured by the Spaniards. He was executed in 1533.

Topa Huallpa *(AD 1532- ?)* was a puppet Inca chosen by Pizarro. Real power rested in the hands of the Spanish.

After the Spanish conquest the Incas held on to a small area to the east of the Andes until 1571.

The social pyramid

Inca society was extremely well-ordered and organized. Everyone, from the Sapa Inca at the top to the peasant farmer at the bottom, knew his position in the social order and the work he was expected to do.

At the top of the pyramid were the Sapa Inca and his Coya, who controlled all power. Below them came the high priest and the commander-in chief of the army. Of a similar rank were the four Apus, the chief officials of the Four Quarters. They were all descendants of previous Sapa Incas. The highest ranks of administrative work fell mainly on members of the Inca family. These judges, generals and chief civil servants formed the privileged ranks, with local administrators below them.

▼ The people at the bottom of the social order were mostly farmers and, on the coasts, fishermen. Records were kept on quipus of everything they produced. These were sent to local governors, who in turn sent the details on to the Inca. Thus at any moment the Inca could learn exactly what was produced in his empire.

The figure on the extreme left was a sorcerer who practised black magic.

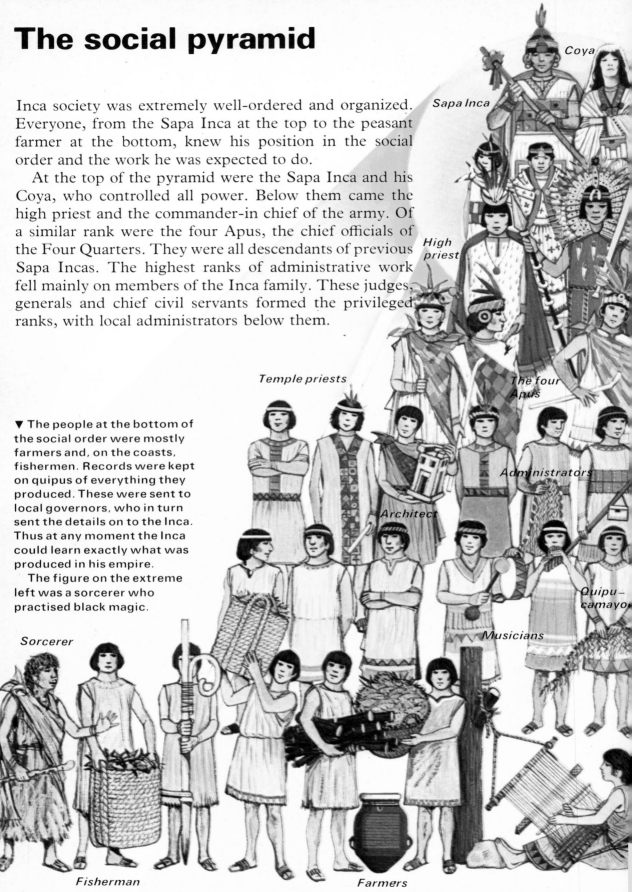

Coya

Sapa Inca

High priest

Temple priests

The four Apus

Administrators

Architect

Quipu–camayo

Musicians

Sorcerer

Fisherman

Farmers

18

Below the privileged classes came lesser administrative officials and specialist craftsmen such as woodworkers, metalsmiths and stonemasons. But the great mass of people forming the basis of Inca society were simple farming families living in the villages, where they grew food crops and looked after livestock.

For most of these people there was little chance of advancement through education. The children did not go to school but were taught all they needed to know by their parents. A few girls were selected to become Sun Virgins while boys conscripted into the army as teenagers might in some cases stay on and become officers. But the schools were open only to the sons of the nobility. Here they were taught Quechua (the Inca language), the laws, religion, the art of war, and how to record and read information from quipus: all the skills that would fit them for their place in the upper levels of society.

rmy
mmander-
-chief

Generals

◄ Junior members of the Inca family held many of the responsible posts in the towns, but other intelligent people could become town officials and heads of villages. Among the middle ranks were architects, engineers, stonemasons, accountants and inspectors, along with lesser officials of the priesthood and army.

▼ The army too had a strict order of rank. All young men were called up to do military service at some stage. The brightest among them might rise to the rank of captain or even higher.

The group with the llama to the left of the soldiers are a herding family wrapped in warm woollen cloaks to keep out the icy mountain winds.

Captains

Artisans

Conscripts

Herding family

19

Clothes and appearance

Although the cloth and decoration of clothes worn by the Inca people varied according to their position in society, the basic style of their dress was always the same. Men wore a simple tunic reaching to just above the knees. Over this they often wore a big loose cloak. On their feet they wore leather sandals or grass shoes. The women dressed in ankle-length gowns, often with a very broad waistband and a cape. On their hair they pinned a folded piece of cloth which hung down their backs.

In the highlands all clothes were made from wool, but in the coastal regions cooler cotton garments were worn.

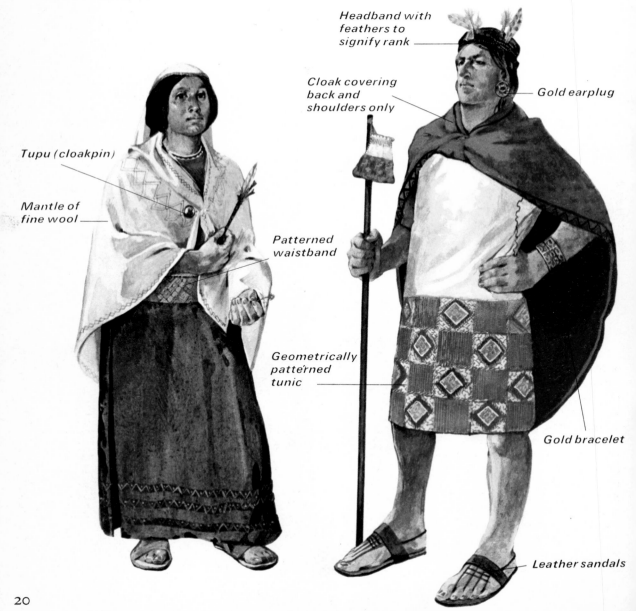

Tupu (cloakpin)

Mantle of fine wool

Headband with feathers to signify rank

Cloak covering back and shoulders only

Gold earplug

Patterned waistband

Geometrically patterned tunic

Gold bracelet

Leather sandals

A captain of the coastal people

A captain of the forest people

A lady of the northern people

▼ The baths of the Inca at Tambo Machay. The Inca nobility took a pride in keeping themselves clean. The baths in the grounds of royal palaces had water piped to them by stone channels or copper pipes.

▲ The popular dress of people from the Four Quarters of Peru. The forest Indians wore little but beads and feathers but the more civilized folk wore fine textiles according to the local fashion. The dress showed where people lived.

◄ An Inca official and his family. Only members of the Inca family were allowed to wear gold ornaments. The square patterns on the man's clothes were high fashion among the Incas. The little boy playing with a top has been out scaring birds; his puma head-dress was part of his hunting gear. The little girl is admiring a pottery whistle. Their clothes made from the wool of the alpaca were warm and comfortable.

Family life

▲ Peruvian farmers today still live by their farmland, in small huts with thatched roofs. As in Inca times, the whole family works, cooks, eats and sleeps in a single room which is often lit only by the light coming through the open doorway.

▶ The interior of a typical Andean home. The woman in the centre is spinning wool. On the right a woman is grinding maize flour. She rocks the heavy stone from side to side to crush the grain. Food was cooked on a clay stove.

Most Andean families lived above or beside farming land, often in small mountain villages. Their houses were built of rough blocks of stone with the cracks plastered with mud. Since nobody would think of taking other people's food or property, there were no doors as we know them. A rough hide or cloth curtain kept out the wind.

There were no beds or chairs in an Andean home. The family slept upon mats and squatted on the floor to work and eat meals. The main meal of the day was eaten in the evening. It generally consisted of a stew made from potatoes, maize, beans and other vegetables, flavoured with hot, spicy seasonings. Maize cobs were also roasted. On special occasions the meat of guinea-pigs was eaten.

Everyone in the family worked hard. They all helped in the fields at planting and harvesting times. But there were many other tasks too. Mother made clothes for all the family from the alpaca wool which she and her daughters had spun and dyed. The men plaited grass for slippers, or cut out llama hide to make strong sandals. Women plaited baskets for carrying loads on their backs. Most of their pots and wooden utensils were home-made.

Give and take

The purpose of government under the Incas was that everybody should help everybody else. All the people worked except for the sick, the very old and the very young. The workers were not paid in money, but what they produced was shared out among them all by a tax system. For example the people usually paid two-thirds of the food they grew in taxes to the state. The food was kept in storehouses, to be distributed to the people in times of need. Throughout society there was a balance between what the people gave to the state and what they received in return.

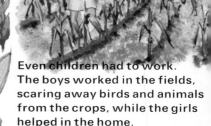

Even children had to work. The boys worked in the fields, scaring away birds and animals from the crops, while the girls helped in the home.

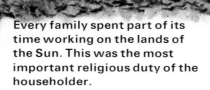

Every family spent part of its time working on the lands of the Sun. This was the most important religious duty of the householder.

An inspector visited the village fields from time to time to assess the amount of grain to be paid in taxes to the state.

Householders might be conscripted for army or community service up to the age of 50. In their absence, neighbours shared their work. Community service included building terraces (right).

When a young couple married, they moved into a house which had been built for them. For the first year they paid no taxes. When a child was born, the family was given more land. As well as weaving all the cloth for the family, the mother also wove cloth for the state.

Harvesting the maize crop. Two thirds of the crop was taken away to be stored in government storehouses, like the ones shown below right.

Once a year inspectors came to select bright, attractive girls to be educated as Sun Virgins.

If the harvest failed, food was sent from the government storehouses (above) so that nobody starved.

In old age people were given light work such as collecting firewood and helping to educate the children. They paid no taxes and were provided with food and clothes by the state.

Growing food

◄ The Incas built irrigation canals which often brought water over long distances. This enabled them to cultivate land which would otherwise have been infertile.

▲ In November the farmers spent much time making sure that the maize was watered.

In Inca times the population of Peru was greater than it is now, so growing enough food was a problem. Every available piece of land had to be cultivated. In the highlands the villagers not only cultivated the river valleys but built irrigated terraces called *andenes* up the hillsides. They built stone walls across the slopes and filled the areas in between with soil so that the mountains looked like giant staircases which turned green whenever the crops sprouted. Mountain streams were diverted to run along the terraces. Here and there were slabs of stone across these water channels. The slabs could be pulled up to let the water run freely and bring life to each patch of land in turn.

Most families farmed fields at several different levels on the mountain slopes. At the top they grew potatoes and crops which could withstand cold. On the middle levels they grew beans and maize, the main food crop. At the bottom they grew fruits and peppers. Thus with careful management they could enjoy foods from all the climatic zones of their empire.

In the coastal region the Incas grew food crops along the fertile river valleys. They diverted the streams along canals to irrigate every possible bit of land. They grew many rich crops, using bird droppings and fish as manure.

▼ June was the time for harvesting the potato crop. The potatoes were stored in a cool dry place.

At planting and harvesting times the whole village would turn out to share the work. Men, women and children all had their tasks to perform.

The farmers cultivated their fields with *tacllas* —footploughs like digging sticks with footrests at the lower end of a long handle. A cast bronze or copper point was usually lashed on at the tip. The stick was driven into the ground, which was then levered up. The women broke up the clods of earth with a broad-bladed wooden hoe with a short handle. Sometimes this had a bronze cutting edge. The boys carried slings to drive away birds and small animals which ate the crops.

▼ Although each family worked an individual piece of ground, neighbours helped each other at harvest time. Here the maize crop is being loaded in baskets and carried to storage bins. A third of the crop was set aside for the Sun and another third for the Inca. Thus there was always enough in the State stores to help out in times of drought.

The high Andes: a herder's life

▲ Llamas were herded on the high plateaux. They were usually looked after by young boys, although in important herding areas, full-time shepherds were sometimes employed.

Animals of the llama family played an important part in the Inca way of life. Alpaca were herded on mountain pastures and their wool provided the cloth worn by most of the people. The wild vicuna was hunted only on the Sapa Inca's command. Its fine silky wool was reserved for his clothes and those of his most important officials. Llamas were occasionally killed for their meat but they were bred mainly as beasts of burden. Small herds of llamas were also kept as sacred animals to be sacrificed at festivals and religious occasions.

Herding was traditionally thought of as a job for young people. Boys armed with slings went up on the high plateaux to look after the animals. They drove off foxes and vultures which were a danger to young animals. They chased the herds from one pasture to another, and saw that they did not trespass on the grounds of other villages. A good deal of time was spent in collecting llama droppings which were used as fuel. Later the village men took the llamas for training as load carriers and sheared the alpacas.

Up in the mountains the men and boys camped in small tents of thick cloth to protect them from the chill weather of the highlands. They wore extra cloaks and woollen caps with ear flaps to keep out the icy winds.

◄ In ancient times, as today, the herders built themselves huts of stone and thatch to give them shelter in the cold air of the highlands. The huts were often very isolated. It was a lonely life with only the animals for company.

► A herd of alpacas at La Raya, the source of the Amazon. The alpaca had a much finer wool than the llama. It was the main material for cloth in ancient times. Even today Peru exports fine alpaca cloth to us.

The round of the year

▼ In August and September the fields were dug and seeded. Men did the ploughing while women planted the maize seed. At the start of the agricultural year, the people prayed for help from the Sun for a good harvest.

August-September

Feast of the Moon

In September the Incas celebrated Coya Raymi, the festival of the Moon and the Queen. During the festivities, warriors danced with torches.

In June the Incas celebrated Inti Raymi, the Feast of the Sun. The Sapa Inca prayed for the sun to rise in the sky the following summer.

June-July

Feast of the Sun

April-May

▲ In June and July, midwinter in the Andes, came the potato harvest. The Incas cultivated many varieties of the potato, which was greatly valued as a source of starch. The tubers were kept in special cool, dry huts until wanted as the basis for stews.

▶ In April and May the maize ears were gathered in, and there was great rejoicing since the winter's food supplies were now secure. All the year's hard work was justified, and the Sun and the Sapa Inca shared in the prosperity and good fortune of the people.

◀ In October and November the young maize plants appeared. Boys were sent to scare off birds and the women cleared the irrigation ditches. The work now was aimed at protecting the growing plants. Life depended on a good maize crop in the months to come.

▼ December and January were the months for tending the growing maize plants and for planting coca for the Incas. When chewed, the leaves of the coca plant acted as a stimulant. Only the priests and the Inca élite were allowed to use this drug.

Magnificent Festival

Capac Raymi, the 'Magnificent Festival' took place in December. The Sapa Inca, dressed in his finery, led the people in Sun worship.

At the Pacha-puchuy (Earth-Ripening) Festival in March, the Inca sacrificed a black llama to atone for the sins of the people.

Earth Ripening

December-January

February-March

▲ In February and March everyone was out protecting the crops from raiding birds and rodents. Even foxes were a menace. This was a crucial time for the farmers since no one could afford to lose much of the crop.

The ocean and the desert

The coasts of Peru were terrible deserts, where in ancient times only the deltas of the short rivers could be cultivated for food. But the sea was full of life. Sealions, seals, whales, dolphins and many varieties of fish swarmed in the cool waters flowing from the south. Fishing lines with hooks were sometimes used to catch the fish but most fishing was done with large seine nets. This type of net had sinkers on the bottom and floats on the top. The fish were caught within the net when the fishermen drew the ends ashore.

Many of the coastal cities sent out great balsa-wood rafts. Each one carried a big cloth sail, but there were also rows of men who sat along the sides and paddled the craft along. Large quantities of goods for exchange were carried up and down along the coast in these vessels.

▼ A balsa raft similar to those used by the Incas. In Inca times steering was done by vertical centre boards pushed between the logs. These light rafts sailed south against the current and then turned to drift back northwards. They carried heavy goods for trade between coastal towns, and supplies for the Inca armies in the southern wars.

PACIFIC OCEAN

Jellyfish

Shrimps

Humboldt current

Bonitos

Booby

Anchovies

Southern sealion

Southern fur seal

▼ The Pacific coast is washed by the cold Humboldt current flowing from the Antarctic. The cold waters welling up from the seabed bring large quantities of plankton and tiny microscopic animals which provide food for many varieties of fish.

Warm ocean currents

Cold ocean currents

Desert

Steppe

Forest

▲ Near the coast the natural vegetation consisted of scrubby bushes. Food crops were grown with the help of irrigation.

▼ Today, as in Inca times, coastal fishermen paddle up and down the coast on boats made of bundles of reeds.

Penguins

Hump-backed whale

Cormorant

Hake

▲ The coastal people caught the fish in nets and hunted the sealions and seals with heavy wooden clubs. Boobies and cormorants were also useful as their droppings, or *guano*, provided a rich source of fertilizer.

An Inca highway

In an area as harsh and rugged as the Andes, the Incas needed a good road system to link up all parts of their empire. Two main roads ran from north to south. These were crossed by hundreds of smaller roads, running east to west, which linked up towns and villages.

On the sandy coasts the roads were not surfaced and were often marked only by lines of tree trunks. In the highlands they were paved with stone or cut into the rocks. These mountain roads often involved great feats of engineering. Sometimes they climbed up like staircases, sometimes they were cut through short tunnels. Where the roads had to cross rivers or mountain gorges, precarious-looking suspension bridges were slung across.

The Incas had not discovered the wheel so all their journeys were made on foot. To help them on their weary way, rest-houses were built every few kilometres on the main roads. Here travellers could camp, cook a meal and feed their herds of llamas. At more frequent intervals there were smaller rest-houses where the *chasquis* awaited their next turn of duty carrying messages.

▶ The Sapa Inca kept in touch with his empire by almost continual travel. He visited every important town and every province in turn. He travelled in a palanquin with rich cushions and a feathered roof. It was usually carried on the shoulders of some of his greatest noblemen.

◄ The Guardian of bridges (top), a very important official who had to inspect the swinging bridges over ravines in the mountains. If he found anything wrong he called out the local work force to make repairs.

Messengers called *Chasqui* runners (bottom) formed an efficient system of communications throughout the empire.

▼ The main traffic on the roads was trains of llamas each carrying bundles of up to 45 kg of goods from place to place. Sometimes there were as many as 200 llamas in such a convoy. They could travel 20 km in one day.

▲ A small group of llamas follow the well-trodden path of an ancient Inca road.

◄ A *Chasqui* hands over his message to the next one. Each messenger ran about a kilometre before handing over to the next runner in the chain and having a brief rest in the little road-side hut built for the purpose. The runners were trained from boyhood and were severely punished if they got a message wrong.

◄ Villagers leave their fields to bow to the Sapa Inca as he passes. It was very rare for the ordinary people to travel. The roads were mostly used by the army and by officials on business.

35

Building

▲ Before construction began, an architect made a model of the finished building. On site he explained his design to a surveyor and a stonemason.

▲ Workmen quarried the giant stones by drilling holes along the rock's fault line, to weaken it, then levering the splintered stones out.

▲ The stones were then transported on a series of rollers or on a carrying frame. Hundreds of workers took part in this back-breaking work.

The Incas delighted in making buildings which fitted into the landscape. In the highland towns the buildings were made of well-cut stones and the outer walls were blank. Doorways and niches sloped inwards slightly towards the top. Most walls too sloped inwards towards the roof. The roofs were of a yellow grass thatch over a metre in thickness. Looked at from a distance, a town seemed almost a part of the surrounding countryside.

The architecture was very formal and simple. Doorways and niches were positioned at regular intervals. Decoration, apart from a few brightly-painted doorways, was reserved for the insides of buildings. But the simplicity was deceptive; it was certainly not to save labour but because the Incas liked it that way. In fact Inca buildings are a miracle of workmanship. Many of their walls of fitted stone were assembled so carefully that a knife blade cannot be forced into their joints. Much Inca stonework has survived earthquakes that have destroyed buildings built since with more elaborate building methods and materials. When disturbed, the Inca stones simply jumped apart and then fell back into position again!

On the coast the architecture was quite different. Chimu buildings were of mud brick, carved and painted with elaborate decoration. But they too blended in well with their surroundings; against the buff, sandy plain and the grey, inland hills they were not conspicuous until one came close to them.

▲ The irregularly-shaped stones were pounded with a stone ball and scrubbed hard with a stone block until their surfaces were smooth.

▲ An earth ramp was used to haul stones up to the higher levels of the wall. The largest stones were placed at the bottom.

▲ A skilled craftsman chiselled the final touches to the fine rectangular blocks used only for the most important parts of buildings.

◀ The front wall of the great Inca fortress of Sacsahuaman. You can get an impression of the size of its massive stones from the figures seated at the bottom of the wall. The building of Sacsahuaman was an enormous undertaking; 20,000 workers were drafted to complete it.

▲ A section of wall showing the two main types of Inca stonework. With the polygonal (many-sided) style of irregularly-shaped stones, each stone was individually shaped and fitted. The rectangular blocks could be finally fitted once they were in position.

Cities and administration

Inca cities were very different from our own, with their mixture of shops, offices and homes. Very few people lived in the city itself; most lived in the surrounding villages and only travelled to the city on business.

In fact the city was almost entirely a centre of government. Here all records for the surrounding districts were kept. Local officials visited their area administrative centres to make reports on the state of the local villages and of the people in general. They were able to call for help in times of disaster and the supplies issued to them were exactly recorded by the *Quipucamayoc*, the Inca 'accountants'.

Every city had a palace for use by the Sapa Inca and the town governor. Nearby, on the city's main roads, were chasqui posts, so that messages could quickly be delivered to all parts of the empire. There were also storehouses in which the tributes of food and clothing were kept. In the artisans' quarters, gold- and silversmiths, carpenters, weavers and other skilled craftsmen were on hand to produce special work for the Inca and for the temples.

An important building was the Sun temple for everywhere the Incas insisted that the Sun god should be worshipped. Near the temple was the *Acllahuasi*, where the Sun Virgins lived far from the public gaze.

▲ A *Quipucamayoc* with one of his quipus, perhaps containing details about goods stored in the palace.

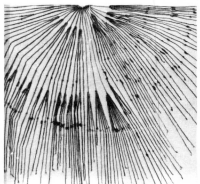

▲ A part of a quipu that has been preserved intact. We know that information was recorded by means of the different coloured strings and the number and position of knots tied in them. But so far no-one has managed to decipher them.

◄ A view of the remains of Tambo Colorado, an important Inca town.

► A plan of a typical Inca town, showing the position of the main government offices.

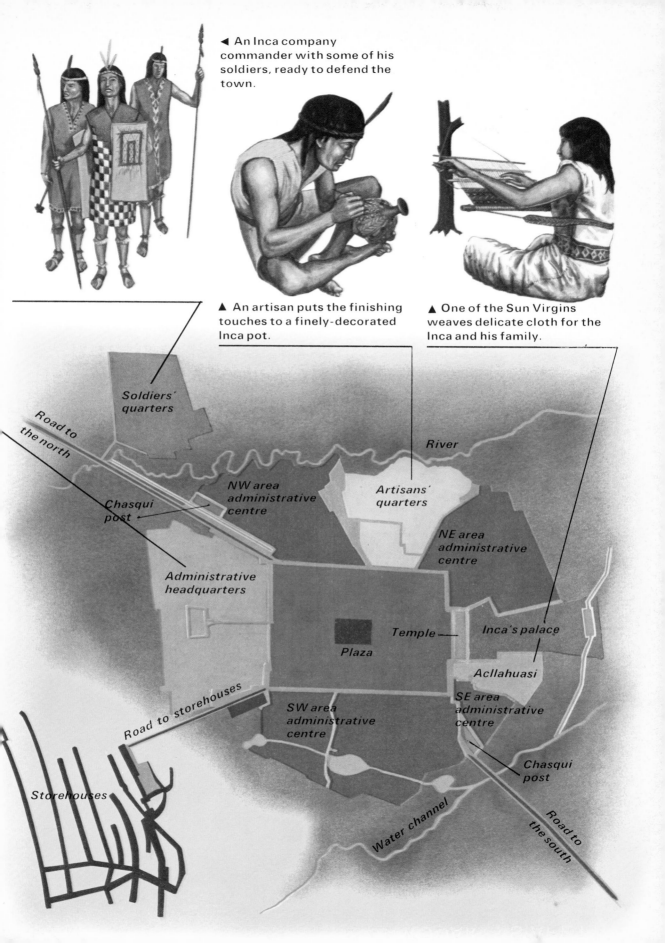

◄ An Inca company commander with some of his soldiers, ready to defend the town.

▲ An artisan puts the finishing touches to a finely-decorated Inca pot.

▲ One of the Sun Virgins weaves delicate cloth for the Inca and his family.

Soldiers' quarters

Road to the north

River

Chasqui post

NW area administrative centre

Artisans' quarters

NE area administrative centre

Administrative headquarters

Temple

Inca's palace

Plaza

Acllahuasi

Road to storehouses

SW area administrative centre

SE area administrative centre

Chasqui post

Storehouses

Water channel

Road to the south

An Inca palace and Acllahuasi

The Sapa Inca had many palaces in important towns all over his empire. These palaces were large complexes of buildings arranged round courtyards. In the innermost part were the living quarters of the Sapa Inca and his Queen. Nearby were other houses for the royal servants. The palace also had great halls and courtyard houses for lodging various nobles held as hostages from other tribes. Other buildings served as houses for the quipus, for clothing and grain, and for military equipment.

▶ The Inca's own living quarters were arranged round a private courtyard, probably with a pleasure garden of flowers. Beyond were the royal baths and a raised platform for ceremonial use.

Storehouses

Reception area

Main gateway to Inca palace

Armoury

▲ The main gateway to the Inca's palace was guarded night and day by a group of soldiers. The main reception area was always bustling with activity. Here the Sapa Inca is being borne out on his litter, to visit another part of his empire.

Soldiers' quarters

At one side of the palace was the Acllahuasi, a convent for the Sun Virgins. Here specially-selected young girls were taught religion and domestic duties by *Mamacuna*, special teaching nuns. The girls learned to spin and weave to a very high standard, to cook fine food and to prepare the chicha used in religious ceremonies. At the age of 13 or 14 they went to Cuzco for the Festival of the Sun, where the Sapa Inca decided their future. Some he chose for his own wives, others he gave away as wives to other members of the Inca family, and the rest served in shrines or themselves became Mamacunas.

Doorway to Acllahuasi

Court for
palace officials
and servants

Inca's
living
quarters

Royal baths

Ceremonial
platform

Gardens

Servants
quarters

Patio of the
Sun Virgins

Gardens

Well

Reception area

▲ The Inca palace (top section)
and Acllahuasi (bottom
section). The buildings,
arranged round courtyards,
were built of stone with roofs
thatched with yellow grass.
Most of the buildings were
single storeyed, although some
had an attic storey. They
consisted of spacious
apartments whose only access
was through the courtyard
onto which they opened.
    The Acllahuasi, like the Inca
palace, was well-guarded. Its
only entrance was through the
doorway at the front.

Spinning and weaving

Very few examples of Inca textiles have been found; most of them have rotted away over the centuries in the damp highland climate. However from the fragments that remain we know that the Incas were skilful weavers.

From an early age all girls learned to spin and weave. They also gathered plants which provided the dyes to colour the alpaca wool. The wool was dyed before it was spun, then woven into sheets of soft, warm cloth which was stitched up to make their clothes. The material was usually plain, although it sometimes had a stripe or simple geometric pattern woven into it.

Material for the clothes of the Inca family was much more elaborate. It was woven by professional weavers and by the Sun Virgins. They used the silky wool of the vicuna which they dyed in brilliant colours. The patterns were complex, geometric designs, often repeated over the entire piece of cloth.

▼ Part of a feather poncho made for a nobleman. The feathers were imported from the jungle.

◄ This Indian woman from Ecuador is spinning yarn in the ancient way. So much yarn was taken up in making a single garment that Inca women were always spinning, even when walking to the town. It took 1200 metres of yarn to make a woman's dress!

de was de tayta y tres años

► A woman weaving a dress length at a back-strap loom. One end of the loom was fastened to a post, the other was attached to a belt which passed round the weaver's waist. She leaned back to tighten the tension and forwards to loosen it to pass the shuttle through the warp. Very complex patterns could be made on this simple loom.

▼ A highly decorated piece of cloth made specially for an Inca. Many of the designs are symbols from Inca mythology and appear as repeating patterns on other Inca shirts.

The craftsman at work

Lost wax casting in gold

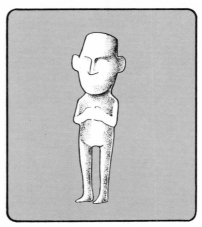

▲ 1 First a solid core of charcoal was made, a little smaller than was wanted for the finished work.

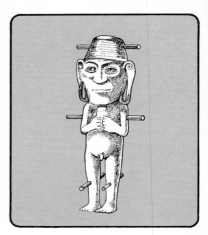

2 The core was coated with beeswax. This was carefully modelled with all the details needed on it.

▲ A 'production line' at the pottery. These distinctively-shaped jars, called *aryballuses,* were made by coiling and then painted with formal designs. They were used for storing and carrying liquids, and some could hold about 16 litres.

In Inca times the craftsman was a much-respected member of the community. He had a special skill which he was expected to use for the good of all. He worked full-time at his craft and was exempt from the usual tribute payments. He and his family were provided for by the state.

The specialist craftsmen made only the finest objects, not those in everyday use. Gold- and silversmiths, for example, made nothing but religious objects and luxury goods for the Sapa Inca and the nobility. Unfortunately very little of their work remains, as most of it was melted down by the Spanish conquerors. But the standard of workmanship was high. The precious metals were either hammered into shape or cast by the lost wax method (see above). Solid casting was rare; even in the Andes gold was not so common that it could be squandered.

The potter's wheel was unknown to the Incas, so all their pottery was made by hand by coiling strips of clay on top of one another to make the required shape. The pots and jars were fired in a furnace and then painted with repetitive geometric designs. The paint used was a liquid clay solution mixed with mineral pigments to make the most common colours—red, purple, cream and black.

Other craftsmen included the stonemasons who built the royal palaces and Sun temples, the woodcarvers who made ceremonial wooden cups called keros and the weavers and embroiderers who made the finest textiles.

3 The whole figure was then covered with clay, with vents left for pouring off the beeswax.

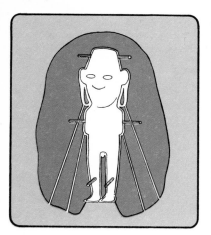

4 The figure was heated and the melted wax poured away. Then molten gold was poured into the empty space.

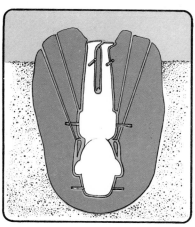

5 When the metal had cooled and solidified, the clay was broken away and the figure cleaned and polished.

▶ **6** The completed figure. Much more complicated openwork designs could also be cast in this way.

▼ This silver alpaca was made by the *repoussé* method, from a sheet of silver. The raised design on the metal was hammered out from the back. The shape of the animal was achieved by hammering over a wooden form. The separate pieces were then soldered together. Golden alpacas were made for the Inca's palace and silver ones for non-Inca nobles. They were probably charms to bring good luck to the household.

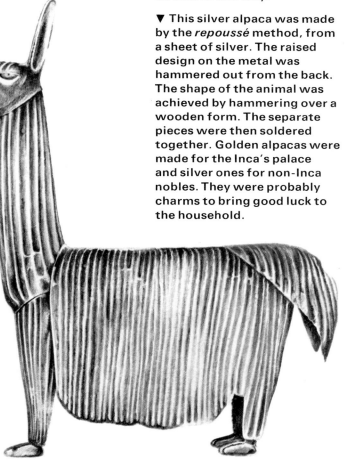

The Sun is God

◄ The Intihuatana at Machu Picchu can just be seen in the very top courtyard of the town.

► The people of the town gather to worship the Sun as it passes overhead. They look on as the high priest pours out an offering of chicha in a golden kero (drinking cup). The Sun Virgins in white assist him in the solemn ritual.

Every important Inca town had a great carved stone, called an Intihuatana, which marked the days on which the Sun passed overhead at noon. At this moment the upright in the centre of the stone cast no shadow.

It was a time for great celebration. The high priest poured out an offering of chicha while the people chanted a hymn to the Sun, thanking him for his warmth and light and for his son the Sapa Inca. After the ceremony the priest and the Sun Virgins departed to leave the people to enjoy themselves. The Inca made a rule that on this great festival the people should be given large vases filled with chicha to drink. They danced and sang and drank until most of them became quiet and fell into a drunken sleep.

Inca sunset: end of an empire

In 1530 a poor Spanish soldier of noble family was asked to get some soldiers together to make an expedition to the South Seas. His task was to discover the truth behind rumours of a land rich in unbelievable quantities of gold. His name was Francisco Pizarro.

After two unsuccessful attempts, Pizarro finally landed with a small force on the Peruvian coast. He found the country in the throes of a civil war between Huascar, the rightful Inca and his half-brother Atahuallpa, who was attempting to usurp his position. Atahuallpa's men had just captured and imprisoned Huascar.

▼ A fresco in Lima Cathedral showing Pizarro, starving on the island of Gallo, sending away those Spaniards who did not wish to accompany him on the conquest of Peru. This was a vital test of the determination of the conquerors to go on to a dangerous trial and victory.

1 The collapse of the Inca empire began with the civil war between the true Inca Huascar and the usurping Atahuallpa, his half-brother.

2 Pizarro marched inland with only 200 men to meet the Incas at Cajamarca. The natives were awestruck by the bearded Spaniards and their horses.

3 When Atahuallpa refused to recognize the Christian faith, the Spaniards captured him and massacred 2000 of his men in a surprise attack.

4 The Spaniards demanded vast quantities of gold as ransom for Atahuallpa's release. Most of the Inca treasures were melted down.

5 Atahuallpa had secretly ordered the death of Huascar. On the pretext that he might cause an uprising, the Spaniards garotted Atahuallpa.

6 Without a leader the Incas had no choice but to submit to the Spaniards. The invaders settled their lands and introduced horses and cattle.

At first the Incas greeted the Spaniards more with curiosity than fear. Huascar's followers on the coast welcomed them, thinking they had come from the heavens to punish Atahuallpa. Atahuallpa himself agreed to meet Pizarro and his men in Cajamarca, confident that with his superior numbers he had nothing to fear. However in a surprise attack Atahuallpa was captured, his men overtaken by the speed of events and confused by the horses and cannons which they had never seen before.

From this moment the Inca empire was doomed. After Atahuallpa's death, a series of powerless Incas were put in charge by Pizarro. Gradually the Spanish settlers took over all the Inca lands. The passing years brought increasing enslavement and degradation of the Incas at the hands of the Spanish government.

▲ The Incas found their Spanish conquerors cruel, even to their children.

Crime and punishment

On the whole the Incas were very law-abiding people. Because they were provided with everything they needed in life, theft was rare. There were no prisons in the whole land. However when people did commit crimes the punishments were often severe.

The worst crimes were murder, insulting the Inca and blaspheming against the gods. These were punishable by death. The usual method of slaying was to throw the villain over a great cliff so that he or she was smashed on the rocks below.

Adultery with one of the Sun Virgins was a particularly dreadful crime; the offending couple were tied hand and foot and hung up by their hair to starve to death. A similar death awaited anyone who made love to any of the Inca's many wives. The man and woman were hung up naked in a public place so that passers-by could laugh at them in their death agony. Insults to the gods were punished by hanging the victim upside down and slashing his belly so that the intestines fell out.

Lesser crimes were punished by the cutting off of hands and feet, or the gouging out of eyes. The unfortunate victims were then kept by the state, and given food and clothing. But every day they were brought to the gates of the nearest town and made to sit with a begging bowl. This was so that everyone could see them and learn what crimes had led to their terrible punishments.

Rebellious tribes were divided up to prevent them from causing further trouble. Half the people were allowed to stay in their old homes, but the other half were deported to distant corners of the empire.

▲ Punishments for adultery were often extremely violent.

▲ An exiled victim is left alone to die among the wild beasts.

Religion

The great gods of the Incas were the powers of nature, especially the Sun, Inti, and the Moon, Quilla. Other important deities were the Thunder and Rainbow gods and the bright planets.

Over them all reigned Viracocha, the Creator. He was both father and mother of the Sun and Moon. He was often thought of as an old man with white hair and beard. He was supposed to be ruler of destiny and invisible; his place in the heavens was a dark area, the 'Coal Sack' in the Milky Way.

The Peruvian Indians were a very superstitious people. They believed many sites and strange objects were inhabited by supernatural forces. They worshipped these holy sites, which were called *huacas*. Huacas included temples, unusually-shaped stones, tombs of ancestors, hills, fountains, springs and caves. Even strange plants or unusual birds were seen as magical and considered to be inhabited by spirits.

Healers used charms for conjuring harmful spirits out of their patients. Any stone with a hole through it, or two twigs growing through each other, were magical healing charms. A sick person was sung over by an enchanter who magicked demons away. Much healing was done by means of herbs, but it was ascribed to the help of the spirits of the plants. It was part of the belief that all nature was one and a sick person must be put in communion with nature to be healed.

The priests watched the stars and kept a complicated calendar which combined solar and lunar rhythms of time. It was used for calculating future good or bad fortune. The many Inca religious festivals also revolved around the rhythms of the Sun and the Moon.

Religious sacrifices were an important part of these festivals. Usually the Incas sacrificed llamas or guinea-pigs, although occasionally human victims were offered up in the most important temples.

The religious order

The high priest in Cuzco was the head of all the priests in the empire. He was generally a brother of the Inca. He had power over all the shrines and temples, appointing their priests. He also presided over all the most important religious ceremonies.

The high priestess was chosen from among the Sun Virgins. With the Coya she led the festivals of the moon, planting etc. She was sworn to a life of chastity.

Priests The ordinary priests served the local temples and huacas. At large shrines there would have been several priests, each with different duties to perform. These included praying, performing sacrifices, interpreting oracles and hearing confessions. At small shrines one priest would have covered all these functions.

Mamacunas or Consecrated Women were nuns dedicated to teaching the young girls who would later become Sun Virgins.

Acllas or Sun Virgins were usually the daughters of leading nobles. They were educated by Mamacunas. They either became wives to the Inca or his nobles, or they spent their lives serving at a shrine or temple. They might themselves become Mamacunas and teach the next generation of Sun Virgins.

Sorcerers were at the bottom of the religious hierarchy, living on the fringes of society. They used black magic to conjure up the spirit powers and obtain messages from them.

Healers were often women. They had a wide knowledge of herbal remedies but also used chants and magical ceremonies to help them in their healing.

The unwritten record

The story of the Incas is not an easy one to unravel. They did not write so they left no books to provide us with clues. Some of the quipus on which they recorded information have been found but so far none have been deciphered except for a few records of planetary movements.

So for a written history of the Incas scholars for a long time had to rely on the stories which Quechua Indians told the Spaniards about their past. The wise old men among them could recite long stretches of history by heart, and Spanish scholars put these legends into books.

Then in 1924 Dr Henri Rivet, a great French expert on ancient America, visited Denmark. There he was shown an ancient book, handwritten in faded ink. It was a History of the Incas with over a thousand pages of illustration. It had been written by an Indian, Guaman Poma de Ayala, the grandson of an Inca administrator. He was brought up in colonial Peru. His mother told him all the stories of the Incas. Guaman Poma sent his book to Philip III as a plea for the Spanish King to take notice of the destruction of the Andean cultures. Later King Philip presented it to the King of Denmark.

But much of what we know about the Incas stems from the work of archaeologists. By their excavations they have uncovered much evidence of Inca and pre-Inca cultures in the form of pottery and metal and stone artefacts. Since many Inca ruins can still be seen, archaeologists can deduce from their architecture what an Inca town may have been like.

▲ Archaeologists excavating a small Inca house.

◀ Guaman Poma as drawn by himself. Many of his drawings of the Incas and their way of life appear throughout this book.

The Incas today

Officially there are no longer any Incas in Peru. Some families among the Quechua-speaking Indians claim descent from the Incas, but there is little proof of this. Yet there are almost certainly strains of Inca family inheritance among these people.

Many of these Indians have left their mountain farms to seek work in the coastal cities. However, life in the cities is not easy and most of the Indians are desperately poor and living in very overcrowded conditions.

The Indians who have remained in the mountain villages keep many of the ancient customs. Many wear warm woollen cloths woven to traditional Inca designs. To help them enjoy life, they have kept up many of the seasonal dances and festivals, though these have been made part of the Christian rituals of life. They have cattle and horses which the Incas never had, but they also still breed guinea-pigs for meat, and shear their alpacas for soft wool. The llama is still used to carry loads.

In the old times most Indian families cultivated three plots of land, one high up, one in the middle heights and one in the valley. Thus they could gather all kinds of crops in their seasons, moving from house to camp as they needed. However recent laws restrict families to ownership of only one plot of land. This means that they may only be able to cultivate one kind of crop, for example maize or potatoes. To obtain the other foodstuffs they need they must now trade amongst themselves.

Many of the Indian villages have mayors and councillors all of Indian descent. Slowly the mountain peoples are learning to live as securely as in ancient times. An English expedition a year ago was led by Dr Ann Kendall to study Inca remains and modern life in the Cusichaca valley near Machu Picchu. They opened up an ancient system of water supply, so that better food supplies could be grown by the local people. The Indians took an active part in the work and now the project is planning more work to help with producing food for the local Indian villages.

On the whole the Indian past of Peru has not been forgotten. Pageants and displays echoing the ancient times are popular. But the Indians are the poorer part of the population. They still have a long way to go before they achieve the security of a well-organized agriculturally-based society that their ancestors enjoyed under the Incas.

▲ These gaily-dressed Indians are playing instruments very similar to those played by Inca musicians.

The story of the Incas

20,000-100 BC

Over 20,000 years ago, hunting peoples who had migrated across the Bering Straits moved south and eventually reached what we now call South America. By 5000 BC some highlanders began cultivating food and making permanent settlements. By 2000 BC the fishing peoples on the coasts too were building more permanent settlements—small towns of mud brick or stones plastered with mud. By 1200 BC the coastal people were cultivating maize, weaving fine cloth and making pottery. At the same time, the first civilization of wide importance, called 'Chavin', had sprung up in the highlands. By 100 BC the northern coast was a kingdom ruled from Moche, and in the south another kingdom was ruled from Nazca.

100 BC-AD 1100

The first highland civilization centred around Tiahuanaco. By AD 800 Tiahuanaco had captured the southern coasts but soon collapsed in civil wars. In AD 1000 Peru was a mass of warring tribes with no strong rulers.

▲ The Chimu kingdom (about AD 1100) was renowned for its gold and silver and textiles.

▲ Pachacuti Inca raises an army to defend Cuzco against invaders.

AD 1100-1438

The Inca Manco Capac had settled in Cuzco. Meanwhile tribes from the north had set up the Chimu kingdom on the northern coast. They built great cities on the rectangular plan with great walled enclosures.

In Cuzco the Incas became stronger. Manco's son Sinchi Roca, like his father, ruled only half of Cuzco and made no moves to make the family more powerful. He encouraged mining and weaving and was a great patron of agriculture. But his son Capac Yupanqui, born late in Sinchi Roca's life, was a warlike chief who extended the Inca dominion over all Cuzco and was a very cruel leader.

Inca Roca was the first to take the title Sapa Inca (Only Inca). Most of his reign was taken up with continuous wars with the Chanca tribes. He was the first Inca to keep land he had conquered.

Yahuar Huaccac succeeded Inca Roca, but was threatened by an alliance of the mountain tribes. His son Viracocha also came under attack but managed to hold back the invaders. However he eventually ran away from Cuzco when the Chanca tribes threatened his kingdom.

AD 1438-1493

Viracocha's son, Pachacuti Inca Yupanqui, succeeded to the throne. The Chanca were beaten and their king killed. Inca Pachacuti then decided to strengthen his position in the highland area he now controlled. He offered peace to the other tribes, giving Inca wives to their chiefs. He rebuilt Cuzco as a capital city and organized a system of government by Inca officials who ruled each tribe as a group of equal citizens of the empire.

As soon as his son Topa Inca Yupanqui was 15, Pachacuti sent him on a career of conquest. At first he conquered the northern lands including most of Ecuador. Topa Inca then took an army out into the Pacific on balsa rafts and came back from distant islands with dark-skinned prisoners and much gold. Next he conquered the Chimu people, incorporating them into the Inca empire.

When Pachacuti Inca retired, his victorious heir came to the throne. Warlike as ever, Topa Inca conquered the forest tribes of the Amazon, defeated rebellious tribes around Lake Titicaca, and took his armies as far south as Chile. Then he returned to Cuzco where he died in 1493.

▲ Topa Inca Yupanqui leads an army into the Pacific on balsas.

▲ Inca warriors were no match for the Spanish soldiers with their superior weapons.

AD 1493-1572

Huayna Capac came to the throne while still a boy. There was much trouble over his accession. He had already married a princess of Quito and had a son Atahuallpa by her. But on becoming Sapa Inca he married his sister; they had a son Huascar.

In the south a tribe of Indian raiders attacked the Chilean frontier of Peru. Among them were some Spaniards, who spread a plague of smallpox. The disease ravaged the land, eventually killing Huayna Capac in 1525.

Huascar Inca took the throne but Huayna Capac had decreed that Atahuallpa was to inherit Quito. In 1532 a civil war started among the half-brothers. Eventually Atahuallpa conquered the whole country and imprisoned Huascar.

In the same year Francisco Pizarro and his small Spanish army landed in Peru. During their first six months they gradually conquered the coastal regions. But eventually they faced the whole Inca army. By a trick they captured Atahuallpa. Two years later the Spaniards had conquered all Tahuantinsuyu. The Inca rulers kept a small kingdom alive for 40 years more, but were never powerful again.

The Inca empire

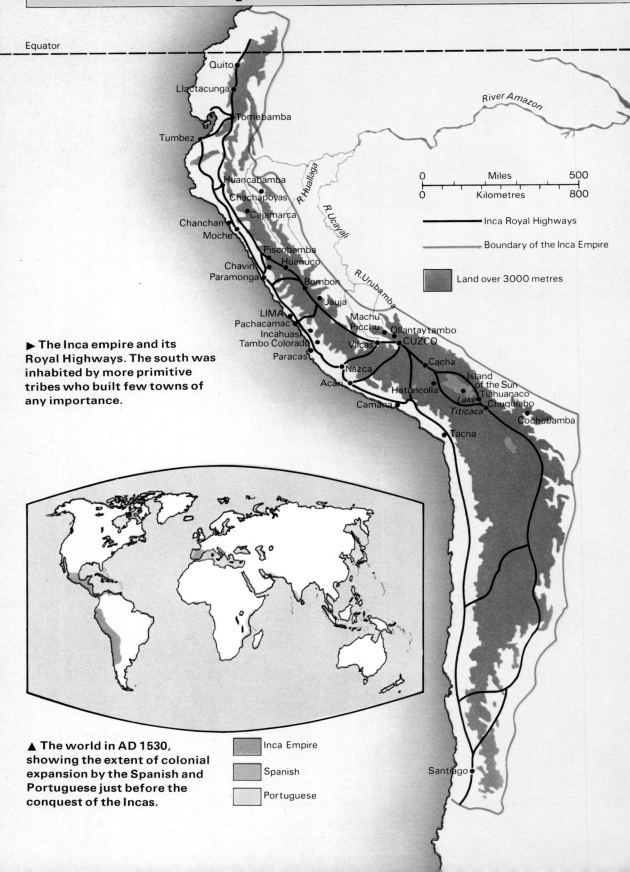

Equator

Quito
Llactacunga
Tomebamba
Tumbez
River Amazon
R. Huallaga
R. Ucavali
Huancabamba
Chachapoyas
Cajamarca
Chanchan
Moche
Piscobamba
Chavin
Huanuco
Paramonga
Bombon
Jauja
R. Urubamba
LIMA
Machu
Picchu
Pachacamac
Ollantaytambo
Incahuasi
Vilcas
CUZCO
Tambo Colorado
Paracas
Cacha
Nazca
Island
of the Sun
Acari
Hatuncolla
Tiahuanaco
Lake
Chuquiabo
Camana
Titicaca
Cochabamba
Tacna
Santiago

	Miles	500
0		
0	Kilometres	800

— Inca Royal Highways
— Boundary of the Inca Empire
Land over 3000 metres

▶ **The Inca empire and its Royal Highways. The south was inhabited by more primitive tribes who built few towns of any importance.**

▲ **The world in AD 1530, showing the extent of colonial expansion by the Spanish and Portuguese just before the conquest of the Incas.**

Inca Empire
Spanish
Portuguese

At the height of their civilization, the Incas ruled an empire over 3,000 kilometres in length and 650 kilometres in breadth. It was divided into four great provinces or *suyu* (quarters): one in the north-east, one in the north-west, one in the south-east and one in the south-west. The whole empire was called Tahuantinsuyu (The Land of the Four Quarters). It was administered from Cuzco, the capital, which was positioned at its approximate centre.

Two main roads, the highland road and the coastal road, ran from north to south of the empire. The provincial capitals and administrative centres were spaced at intervals along these roads. Lesser roads ran from east to west, linking the highland capitals to important coastal towns.

The Inca empire was made up of very different tribes. Highly organized coastal states such as the Chimu were easily absorbed. But the more primitive forest tribes never became fully integrated.

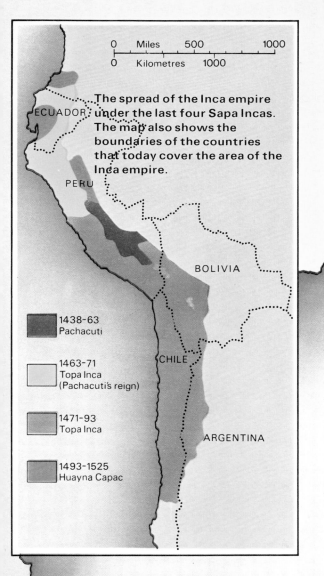

The spread of the Inca empire under the last four Sapa Incas. The map also shows the boundaries of the countries that today cover the area of the Inca empire.

- 1438-63 Pachacuti
- 1463-71 Topa Inca (Pachacuti's reign)
- 1471-93 Topa Inca
- 1493-1525 Huayna Capac

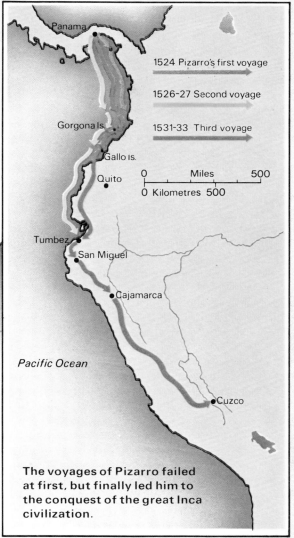

1524 Pizarro's first voyage

1526-27 Second voyage

1531-33 Third voyage

The voyages of Pizarro failed at first, but finally led him to the conquest of the great Inca civilization.

World history AD 1100 to 1600

	Incas	Europe	Asia
AD 1100	The Inca family under their leader Manco Capac settle in the highland town of Cuzco. At first they rule only half of Cuzco and make no attempt to become more powerful.	In Italy independent city-states emerge. Great trading centres are established in the north German cities, while Constantinople becomes the centre of European culture. Universities are set up at Oxford and in Paris.	Under Genghis Khan the Mongol Empire is extended from Manchuria to the Caucasus and the invasion of Russia is begun. Under the Sung Dynasty in China, fine porcelain is made.
AD 1200	Inca dominion is extended over the whole of Cuzco. Small conquests are made in the surrounding region but these are not organized; the Incas simply carry out periodical raids on villages when the people seem to pose a threat or when an occasion presents itself.	In England King John signs the Magna Carta. The Franciscan order is founded by St Francis. Poland and Hungary are invaded by the Mongols. Wales is conquered by Edward I but Scotland revolts and sides with France.	The Mongols invade Russia. They are defeated in the west but control east Russia. Under Genghis Khan they also invade China. Later Kublai Khan establishes a Mongol capital at Peking and eventually makes himself emperor of all China. Marco Polo travels to his court.
AD 1300	Inca Roca becomes the first leader to take the title Sapa Inca. Fighting with neighbour-hood tribes becomes more organized and the Incas begin to hold on to land they have conquered.	At the Battle of Bannockburn the English are defeated by the Scots. The Hundred Years' War between England and France breaks out. The Black Death destroys half Europe's population. Portugal becomes independent from Spain.	The central state of Moscow is created under the Mongols but eventually they are driven out. Gunpowder is first used for military ends. The Mongols are driven out of China and the Ming dynasty begins. The Mongols invade India.
AD 1400	The greatest period in the history of the Inca civilization. Under the leadership of first Pachacuti Inca Yupanqui and later Topa Inca Yupanqui, the Inca empire expands rapidly.	French armies led by Joan of Arc defeat the English. Later Joan is burnt at the stake. The Italian Renaissance flourishes, with such artists as da Vinci, Michelangelo and Botticelli. Gutenberg invents the printing press. The Hapsburg family rule central Europe.	Tamerlane's Central Asian Empire collapses. India, Persia and Afghanistan become independent. In India religious conflict breaks out between Hindus and Moslems. Vasco da Gama reaches India. In Japan civil war breaks out.
AD 1500 / **AD 1600**	In the south Spaniards among an Indian raiding party bring small-pox to the country. Civil war between the rightful Sapa Inca Huascar and his half-brother Atahuallpa threatens the unity of the empire. Pizarro and his men conquer the Incas and rule the country as a Spanish province.	The Moors are finally expelled from Spain. Luther's attack on the Catholic Church marks the start of the Protestant Reformation. Copernicus first proposes a universe centred round the Sun. Drake sails round the world and destroys the Spanish Armada.	Ivan the Terrible of Russia conquers Siberia. India is united in a great civilization under the Moguls. Portugal trades with India and Japan. The Dutch begin a spice trade with the Spice Islands.

Africa	Near East	America	
			AD 1100
he Fatimid dynasty rules gypt. These are Moslems who e hostile to the Seljuk Turks it who support them in their ght to take back Jerusalem om the Crusaders. Saladin ecomes ruler of Egypt and onquers Jerusalem.	The Crusaders establish states along the coast of Syria, defended by strong castles. They take Jerusalem but lose it to Saladin, the ruler of Egypt and Syria. Saladin allows Christian pilgrims to visit the holy shrines.	The Aztecs, one of the Chichimec group of Indians, move into the valley of Mexico. They move from one site to another in their quest for land in which to settle.	
			AD 1200
trade treaty is agreed between ypt and Venice. The fifth rusade in Egypt is defeated. ouis IX of France is killed in the al (9th) Crusade. he Mongols try unsuccessfully invade Egypt. he Mandingo empire is unded. Its centre is at mbuktu.	The Crusaders win back Jerusalem but are once again defeated. They lose their Crusader states and are compelled to beat a retreat to Cyprus. The Near East is invaded by the Mongols, who destroy Baghdad.	City states compete for power throughout Mexico. The Aztecs settle at Chapultepec but are defeated and enslaved by the Tepanec. Some escape to the islands of Lake Texcoco. In the American south-west, raids by Navaho Indians destroy the Cliff Dweller culture.	
			AD 1300
he Mandingo empire unites Vest Africa. he Black Death spreads to gypt. lexandria is taken by the ing of Cyprus. slave trade is developed along e east coast by the Arabs.	The Ottoman empire is established under the Turks. They conquer Greece and extend their influence throughout eastern Europe.	The Maya civilization on the Yucatan Peninsula is torn apart by civil war. Their civilization begins to decline. The Aztecs are driven out by the Tepanecs. They join the rest of their tribe and found their island capital of Tenochtitlan.	
			AD 1400
West Africa the Portuguese stablish a trading post on the uinea coast. They convert the ng of Congo to Christianity. artholomew Diaz reaches the ape of Good Hope. Vasco da ama rounds the Cape.	Turkish lands are invaded and the Turkish army destroyed by the Mongols. In Greece the Turks recover and invade Hungary. They capture Constantinople and rename it Istanbul.	Aztec armies begin the conquest of the Valley. They amass great wealth and build a powerful empire. Montezuma 1 is elected as their Chief Speaker. Christopher Columbus discovers the New World. John Cabot lands in Newfoundland and claims it for England.	
			AD 1500
ozambique is founded by the ortuguese. They explore the iver Zambesi. he British start exporting aves from West Africa to merica. unis is captured from the Turks the Spanish. ortuguese missionaries settling Ethiopia are expelled.	The Turkish empire is extended to north-west India and Arabia. At the Battle of Lepanto Turkish supremacy at sea is broken by Spain and Venice.	The Inca, Maya and Aztec empires are vanquished by the Spaniards. English, French and Dutch explorers reach the New World. Sir Francis Drake stakes a claim on California for England.	
			AD 1600

Glossary

alpaca animal of the llama family with fine wool used for clothing.
andenes cultivation terraces built along the mountainsides.
apus local governors of the Four Quarters of Tahuantinsuyu.
archaeology the study of the past through the excavation and examination of historical remains.
balsa sailing raft made from light balsa wood.
Coya the Queen, always a sister of the Inca. Her son was the true heir to the position of Sapa Inca.
chasquis running messengers.
Chavin ancient culture which lasted from 900 BC to 200 BC.
chicha a kind of beer made from fermented maize.
Chimu a kingdom on the north coast which was powerful from AD 1100 to AD 1450.
Cuzco the Inca capital, known as the Navel of the Earth.
garotte execute by strangling.
huaca any sacred or magical object.
Inca the ruling family in ancient Peru.
Inti the Sun God, giver of food and strength.
Mamacunas teaching nuns for the Sun Virgins.
Mochica ancient coastal civilization dating from 100 BC to AD 600.
Paramonga a great mud-brick fortress built by the Chimu.
Quilla the Moon Goddess.
quipu a fringe of knotted strings used for keeping records.
Quipucamayoc recorder of information on quipus.
Sapa Inca the Only Emperor of the people.
Sun Virgins girls dedicated to the service of the Sun.
tacllas digging sticks with a footrest.
Tahuantinsuyu Inca name for their empire meaning 'The Four Quarters'.
Tiahuanaco highland culture dating from AD 600 to 1000.
vicuna small, wild member of the llama family, which provided fine glossy wool for the clothes of the Inca and his nobles.

Index

60